What if you were a Master Creator?

What if you were so good at creating, you could create anything you wanted from seemingly nothing at all?

What if you were so good at creation, creation started becoming dull? Although you had the admiration of world after world (some of which you helped create), you began to miss the challenge you felt earlier in your creative career.

So, Master Creator that you are, you created a button marked "Greater Challenge."

You considered all that might be contained in the concept of "Greater Challenge," decided Greater Challenge would probably provide some of the excitement and satisfaction you missed from your apprentice days, took a deep breath, pushed the button . . .

. . . and found yourself where you are now—feeling what you're feeling now, thinking what you're thinking now, with everything in your life precisely the way it is now—reading this book.

Books by Peter McWilliams

LOVE 101:
To Love Oneself Is the Beginning of a Lifelong Romance*

LIFE 102:
What to Do When Your Guru Sues You

You Can't Afford the Luxury of a Negative Thought:
A Book for People with Any Life-Threatening Illness—Including Life*

Focus on the Positive:
The You Can't Afford the Luxury of a Negative Thought Workbook

LIFE 101:
Everything We Wish We Had Learned About Life In School—But Didn't*

DO IT! Let's Get Off Our Buts*

The Portable LIFE 101

How to Heal Depression*

How to Survive the Loss of a Love*

*These titles are also available in unabridged audio format.

The Portable
DO IT!

172 essential excerpts plus 190 quotations
from the #1 *New York Times* bestseller
DO IT! Let's Get Off Our Buts

by Peter McWilliams

Prelude Press
8159 Santa Monica Boulevard
Los Angeles, California 90046
1-800-LIFE-101

ISBN 0-931580-81-1

Book design by Victoria Marine

Printed in the United States of America by Vaughan Printing

Introduction

(a very short one, in keeping with the brevity of this book)

The Portable DO IT! contains 172 essential excerpts from the text of the much longer book *DO IT! Let's Get Off Our Buts*. As Blaise Pascal once penned to a friend, "If I had more time, I would write a shorter letter." When I wrote the original *DO IT!*, I didn't have the time, so it was a longer book. I've now taken the time and created this more portable version.

If you read the full-sized *DO IT!* (I can't call it *"The Stationary DO IT!"* because doing it is never stationary), *The Portable DO IT!* will be a review, a traveling companion while you're fulfilling your dreams. If you haven't read the full-sized *DO IT!*, *The Portable DO IT!* will be a preview (a painless one, I trust). Also taken from the original *DO IT!* are 190 quotations from famous doers, past and present.

I might repeat to myself, slowly and soothingly,
a list of quotations beautiful from minds profound—
if I can remember any of the damn things.

DOROTHY PARKER

If you want to explore an idea more fully, at the bottom of each page, in the center, is a small number. This is the page number in the full-sized *DO IT!* from which the excerpt was taken. Turning to that page in the original *DO IT! Let's Get Off Our Buts* will give you a broader perspective on the excerpted thought.

Thanks for reading, and enjoy *doing it!*

Peter McWilliams

Page number from
the original *DO IT!*
will appear here

I was going to buy a copy of
The Power of Positive Thinking,
and then I thought:
What the hell good would that do?

RONNIE SHAKES

The Portable
DO IT!

*To achieve your goal,
your life may sound
like a perfume counter—
full of Passion and Obsession,
leading to Joy.*

1

We all have a dream, a heart's desire. Most have more than one. Some of us have an entire entourage. This is a book of practical suggestions for discovering (or rediscovering) those dreams, choosing which ones to pursue, and achieving them.

Properly, we should read for power.
Man reading should be man intensively alive.
The book should be a ball of light in one's hand.

EZRA POUND

3

2

By pursuing any *one* of our dreams, we can find fulfill-ment. We don't need to pursue them all.

> *As Miss America,*
> *my goal is to bring peace*
> *to the entire world*
> *and then*
> *to get my own apartment.*

JAY LENO

3

3

We don't have to *achieve* a dream in order to find fulfillment—we need only actively *pursue* the dream to attain satisfaction.

> *Regret for the things we did*
> *can be tempered by time;*
> *it is regret for the things we did not do*
> *that is inconsolable.*

SYDNEY J. HARRIS

3

4

By living our dream, we can contribute not only to ourselves, but to everyone and everything around us. And yet, most people are not pursuing their dreams.

> *There are some people*
> *that if they don't know,*
> *you can't tell them.*

LOUIS ARMSTRONG

3

5

When we're not pursuing our dreams, we spend our time and abilities pursuing the things we *think* will make us happy, the things we *believe* will bring us fulfillment: the new house, the new car, the new cashmere jump suit.

> *You can't get enough
> of what you don't really want.*

3

6

Many people are so far away from living their dream that *they have forgotten what their dream truly is.*

> *Many of life's failures are*
> *people who did not realize*
> *how close they were to success*
> *when they gave up.*

THOMAS EDISON

4

7

It is sad. It is unnecessary. It is wasteful. And yet, it's so common an ailment that it's become a cliché. We have abandoned our heart's desire—and somewhere, deep down, we know it. Even if we don't remember quite what it is—we miss it.

"Let's Go."
"Yes, let's go."
Stage direction: They do not move.

LAST LINES OF
WAITING FOR GODOT
SAMUEL BECKETT

4

8

You may find the first part of this book depressing. I'm going to explain why most people aren't living their dreams—and I'm not going to pull any punches. It's not a pretty picture.

> *Facts do not cease to exist*
> *because they are ignored.*

WILLIAM S. BURROUGHS

> *You have everything but one thing: madness.*
> *A man needs a little madness or else—*
> *he never dares cut the rope and be free.*

ZORBA THE GREEK

11

*There are many who are living
far below their possibilities
because they are continually handing over
their individualities to others.
Do you want to be a power in the world?
Then be yourself.
Be true to the highest within your soul
and then allow yourself to be governed
by no customs or conventionalities
or arbitrary man-made rules
that are not founded on principle.*

RALPH WALDO TRINE

9

Why aren't we living our dreams? Because there is something we are trained to honor more than our dreams: **the comfort zone**.

We act as though comfort and luxury
were the chief requirements of life,
when all that we need to make us happy
is something to be enthusiastic about.

CHARLES KINGSLEY

4

10

The comfort zone is all the things we have done often enough to feel comfortable doing again. Whenever we do something new, it falls outside the confines of the comfort zone. In even contemplating a new action, we feel fear, guilt, unworthiness, hurt feelings, and/or anger—all those emotions we generally think of as "uncomfortable."

*The only thing I can't stand
is discomfort.*

GLORIA STEINEM

5

11

When we feel uncomfortable enough long enough, we tend to feel discouraged (a form of exhaustion), and we return to thoughts, feelings, and actions that are more familiar, more practiced, more predictable—more, well, comfortable.

> *It is hard to fight an enemy*
> *who has outposts in your head.*
>
> SALLY KEMPTON

5

12

The irony is that the feelings we have been taught to label "uncomfortable" are, in fact, among the very tools necessary to fulfill our dreams. As it turns out, the bricks used to build the walls of the comfort zone are made of gold.

> *Each handicap*
> *is like a hurdle in a steeplechase,*
> *and when you ride up to it,*
> *if you throw your heart over,*
> *the horse will go along, too.*

LAWRENCE BIXBY

5

13

We no longer believe in Santa Claus, but we still believe that "being uncomfortable" is reason enough not to do something new. The Easter Bunny hopped out of our lives years ago, yet we still let "what other people might think" affect our behavior. The tooth fairy was yanked from our consciousness long before adolescence, but we still feel we can justify any personal failure by blaming someone or something outside ourselves.

We're all in this alone.

LILY TOMLIN

5

14

Most people are drifting along in a childish sleep. To live our dreams, we must wake up.

Men stumble over the truth from time to time,
but most pick themselves up and hurry off
as if nothing happened.

SIR WINSTON CHURCHILL

Losing my virginity was a career move.

MADONNA

6

15

F. Scott Fitzgerald met Joan Crawford at a Hollywood party. He told her that he had been hired to write the screenplay for her next film. She looked him straight in the eye and said, "Write hard, Mr. Fitzgerald, write hard."

Imagine that I am looking you straight in the eye and saying, "Dream big, dear reader, dream big."

If you're not playing a big enough game,
you'll screw up the game you're playing
just to give yourself something to do.

8

16

The truth is, pursuing a Big Dream of your own choosing is the same amount of work as gathering more and more of the things you don't really want. You're going to spend the rest of your life doing *something*—it might as well be something *you* want to do.

> *Ours is a world where people*
> *don't know what they want*
> *and are willing to go*
> *through hell to get it.*

DON MARQUIS

8

17

The willingness to do creates the ability to do.

Where does the willingness come from?

From you.

As Joni Mitchell pointed out, "It all comes down to you."

I certainly agree, and would only add, "It all comes down to *do.*"

Every creator painfully experiences the chasm
between his inner vision and its ultimate expression.

ISAAC BASHEVIS SINGER

9

*This is the true joy of life,
the being used for a purpose
recognized by yourself as a mighty one;
and being thoroughly worn out
before you are thrown on the scrap heap;
the being a force of nature
instead of a feverish selfish little clod
of ailments and grievances complaining
that the world will not devote itself
to making you happy.*

GEORGE BERNHARD SHAW

18

The reason we aren't living our dreams is *inside ourselves*. We *pretend* it's people, things, and situations *outside ourselves* that are to blame.

Always listen to experts.
They'll tell you what
can't be done and why.
Then do it.

ROBERT HEINLEIN

11

19

When we know that the *cause* of something is in ourselves, and that we (ourselves) are one of the few things in this universe that we have the right and the ability to change, we begin to get a sense of the choices we really do have, an inkling of the power we have, a feeling of being in charge—of our lives, of our future, of our dreams.

They always say that time changes things,
but you actually have to change them yourself.

ANDY WARHOL

11

20

BUT—that three-letter, four-letter word. "But" usually means: "ignore all that good-sounding stuff that went before—here comes the truth." You might even consider BUT an acronym for ***B**ehold the **U**nderlying **T**ruth.* (And BUTS can be shortened to BS.)

*Do or do not.
There is no try.*

YODA

17

21

The naked "but" is what we use when ignoring our own good advice. When ignoring the unbearably good advice of others, we use the hyphenated version: "yes-but." When we argue for our limitations, we get to keep them. *Yes-but* means, "Here come the arguments for my limitations." Or, if you favor acronyms . . .

*YES-BUT = **Y**our **E**valuation is **S**uperb—*
***B**ehold the **U**nderlying **T**ruth.*

*Advice is what we ask for when we already
know the answer but wish we didn't.*

ERICA JONG

19

22

In life, we have either reasons or results—excuses or experiences, stories or successes. We either have what we want, or we have ironclad, airtight, impenetrable reasons why it was not even *marginally possible* to get it.

Success is simply
a matter of luck.
Ask any failure.

EARL WILSON

21

23

We've been programmed to use one of the most power-ful tools *at* our disposal—the mind—*for* our disposal. Rather than dispose of the barriers to our dreams, the mind disposes of the *dreams*.

> *In the choice between*
> *changing one's mind*
> *and proving there's*
> *no need to do so,*
> *most people get busy*
> *on the proof.*

JOHN KENNETH GALBRAITH

21

24

In the amount of time it takes for the mind to invent a good excuse, the mind could have created an alternative way of achieving the result—rendering excuse-making unnecessary.

Quit now, you'll never make it.
If you disregard this advice,
you'll be halfway there.

DAVID ZUCKER

21

25

Let's take a closer look at fear, guilt, unworthiness, hurt feelings, anger, and discouragement. (Just what you wanted, huh?)

> *Minds, like bodies,*
> *will often fall into*
> *a pimpled, ill-conditioned state*
> *from mere excess of comfort.*

CHARLES DICKENS

26

Because it's so common, **fear** has many other names: apprehension, misgiving, trepidation, dread, horror, phobia, terror, alarm, consternation, foreboding, qualm, suspicion, fret, uneasiness, distress, panic, worry.

I'm a paranoiac, baby,
so I hope you don't make the mistake
of laboring under the false impression
that you are talking to a sane person.

TENNESSEE WILLIAMS

31

27

Physically, we tend to feel fear in the area we generally call the stomach. Although it's lower than the biological stomach (more in the area of the lower abdomen), for the sake of locating fear—and going along with the popular use of the word—I'll define "the stomach" as a large, circular area with the navel at its center. (Guilt hangs out there too.)

> *Fear is the main source of superstition,*
> *and one of the main sources of cruelty.*
> *To conquer fear is the beginning of wisdom.*
>
> BERTRAND RUSSELL

31

28

Someone once described FEAR in an acronym: *False Expectations Appearing Real*. For the most part, what we fear is not real—it is merely our mind imagining something awful that has not yet happened.

Fear is pain arising from the anticipation of evil.

ARISTOTLE

To him who is in fear, everything rustles.

SOPHOCLES

31

29

Seldom do we do the thing we fear, so we seldom discover whether or not our projection of disaster was accurate. In fact, when we *don't* do the thing we are afraid of, we breathe a sigh of relief as *though it actually would have taken place.* "That was a *close* one!" we say, even though we never actually got *close* to anything but a string of our own negative thoughts. Fear breeds lack of experience; lack of experience breeds ignorance (*ignore*-ance); ignorance breeds more fear. It is a vicious circle.

*You can't expect to hit the jackpot
if you don't put a few nickels in the machine.*

FLIP WILSON

32

30

Put another way, fear is interest paid on a debt you may not owe.

> *Fear is that little darkroom*
> *where negatives are developed.*
>
> MICHAEL PRITCHARD

33

31

Guilt is the anger we feel toward ourselves when we think we've done something "wrong." The trouble is, most of us haven't explored what *we* think is truly "right" and "wrong" in years—maybe ever.

> *The only reason I feel guilty*
> *about masturbation*
> *is that I do it so badly.*
>
> DAVID STEINBERG

37

32

The process of limitation and immobility is *fear before* we do something new, and *guilt after.* (Maybe that's why they're both felt in the stomach area.) Guilt is the remorse—the shame, the regret—we feel at having done something "different." We feel so bad we promise ourselves, "I'll never do that again!" even if it's the very thing we need to do, over and over again.

Last night at twelve I felt immense,
But now I feel like thirty cents.

GEORGE ADE
1902

37

33

Guilt can rewrite the *memory* of an experience. We may do something new and enjoy doing it (or the result of doing it), but guilt will actually convince us that we didn't like it (or got nothing from it.) We can say, "I'm not going to do that again; I didn't really like it, and *believe it*—although, in fact, the experience itself (not the fear before the experience or the guilt after, but the *actual experience*) was enjoyable (or profitable).

If you're going to do something wrong, at least enjoy it.

LEO ROSTEN

38

34

Unworthiness is the deep-seated belief that tells us we're undeserving, not good enough, inadequate, and fundamentally deficient.

> *You have no idea*
> *what a poor opinion*
> *I have of myself—*
> *and how little I deserve it.*

W. S. GILBERT

41

35

Unworthiness is the primal doubt we feel in the pit of our stomach when we consider living a dream.

"Don't try it," unworthiness warns. "Don't even *think* about it."

And so, we don't even think about it. Our mind goes off on one distraction after another—*anything* rather than having to face even the possibility of our own elemental inadequacy.

Our doubts are traitors, and make us lose the good
we oft might win by fearing to attempt.

SHAKESPEARE

41

36

Physically, unworthiness resides in the area of the solar plexus—an area just below the breast bone where the rib cage forms an inverted "V". In some Eastern traditions, they call this the center of *Chi*, a fundamental point for focusing energy and moving ahead in life. Unworthiness inhibits that energy.

The wonderful thing about saints is that they were human.
They lost their tempers, scolded God,
were egotistical or testy or impatient in their turns,
made mistakes and regretted them.
Still they went on doggedly blundering toward heaven.

PHYLLIS McGINLEY

42

37

One of the most popular of unworthiness's comments, however, is, upon hearing of our own good fortune, "I don't believe it! That's too good to be true!" It's often spoken with such enthusiasm—and such self-limitation—that the good that's "unbelievable" soon disappears.

> *The world is moving so fast these days*
> *that the man who says*
> *it can't be done*
> *is generally interrupted*
> *by someone doing it.*

HARRY EMERSON FOSDICK

43

38

When we don't get what we want from others, when they fail to keep their promises, when they let us down, we often have **hurt feelings**.

Even deeper (and more frequent) are the times we have let *ourselves* down. That hurts too.

> *There is no security on this earth,*
> *there is only opportunity.*

GENERAL DOUGLAS MACARTHUR

45

39

A common "cover-up" for hurt is **anger**. We blame whatever or whoever let us down, and we get *steamed*. ("How *dare* you!" Why *didn't* you?") Some people have anger as the *automatic response* to disappointment. In almost all cases, however, hurt is just underneath.

> *I buy women shoes,*
> *and they use them*
> *to walk away from me.*
>
> MICKEY ROONEY

45

40

How much greater are our imagination and desires than our physical abilities to fulfill them. The result of all this letdown is often hurt feelings—sadness, loss, grief.

I know a man who gave up smoking,
drinking, sex, and rich food.
He was healthy right up to the time he killed himself.

JOHNNY CARSON

Your request for no MSG was ignored.

FORTUNE COOKIE

45

41

After enough hurt and anger, people tend to decide, "I'm not going to do anything that causes me any more pain." That would, of course, include any dream-fulfillment behavior.

*You have to leave the city of your comfort
and go into the wilderness of your intuition.
What you'll discover will be wonderful.
What you'll discover will be yourself.*

ALAN ALDA

45

42

Over time, the result of all this fear, guilt, unworthiness, hurt feelings, and anger is **discouragement**. (Discouragement promotes inaction, and inaction guarantees failure—a life of not living our dreams.)

> *Discouragement is simply
> the despair of
> wounded self-love.*
>
> FRANÇOIS DE FÈNELON

47

43

It's hard to imagine anything more pernicious—and effective—than discouragement. Although we, as adults, have the power we didn't have as children to pursue our dreams, discouragement keeps us from using it.

> *Basically, my wife was immature.*
> *I'd be at home in the bath*
> *and she'd come in*
> *and sink by boats.*

WOODY ALLEN

47

44

Our parents (or whoever raised us) *loved* us—in the most fundamental sense of that word. Maybe they didn't hug us all we wanted, but we are alive today because they (at least minimally) *fed* us.

> *I learned the way a monkey learns—*
> *by watching its parents.*
>
> QUEEN ELIZABETH II

45

The primary reasons parents don't raise their children free from trauma are

1. Parents don't know any better.
2. Children learn by example.
3. Parents have other things to do besides raising children (like dealing with money, each other, and life).
4. Who on earth knows what a child needs when?

If you want a place in the sun,
you must leave the shade of the family tree.

OSAGE SAYING

57

46

The bad news about the comfort zone: The comfort zone is never static. It is dynamic—always expanding or contracting. If you're not consciously expanding your comfort zone, it contracts.

> *He not busy being born is busy dying.*
>
> BOB DYLAN

47

The worst news about the comfort zone: The comfort zone is not just a collection of "uncomfortable" emotions— it has its own personality, character, and individuality. It is a complex psychological-physiological being unto itself.

> *Don't try to take on a new personality;*
> *it doesn't work.*
>
> RICHARD NIXON

48

Many don't see the comfort zone as a limitation at all. They call it "intuition," "morality," or "conscience." Some connect it with *religion*—they think the limiting rantings of the comfort zone are the voice of God.

(I won't even discuss what happens when these people put their self-limitations on others—by force, if necessary. Well, take a look at history; take a look *around!*)

A great many people think they are thinking when they are merely rearranging their prejudices.

WILLIAM JAMES

77

49

The comfort zone knows us intimately and hits us at our weakest point. It wouldn't dream of using an excuse we could see through. It uses the reasons we find reasonable, the rationales we find rational (the "rational lies"), the realizations we find most real ("real lies"). It takes our greatest aspirations and turns them into excuses for not bothering to aspire.

> *My idea of an agreeable person*
> *is a person who agrees with me.*
>
> BENJAMIN DISRAELI

77

Good behavior is the last refuge of mediocrity.

HENRY S. HASKINS

*If you have a job without aggravations,
you don't have a job.*

MALCOM FORBES

50

The even worse news about the comfort zone: To the degree we're not living our dreams, our comfort zone has more control of us than we have over ourselves.

Human beings yield in many situations,
even important and spiritual and central ones,
as long as it prolongs one's well-being.

ALEXANDER SOLZHENITSYN

79

*One can never consent to creep
when one feels
an impulse to soar.*

HELEN KELLER

51

The very worst news about the comfort zone: In order to truly master the comfort zone, we must learn to love it.

> *Love your enemies*
> *just in case*
> *your friends turn out to be*
> *a bunch of bastards.*

R. A. DICKSON

81

52

The good news about the comfort zone: All the energy that makes up the comfort zone is *yours*.

Men are born to succeed, not to fail.

HENRY DAVID THOREAU

*If you want a quality,
act as if you already had it.
Try the "as if" technique.*

WILLIAM JAMES

85

53

We are built for success. We're programmed for failure, perhaps, but we're built for success.

Use your weaknesses;
aspire to the strength.

SIR LAURENCE OLIVIER

83

54

We play isometrics with our feelings and our attitudes. A certain feeling arises. An attitude says we shouldn't have that feeling and pushes it down. It's like arm wrestling with ourselves—we can expend a lot of energy and work diligently, but not much is accomplished.

My grandmother started walking
five miles a day when she was sixty.
She's ninety-five now,
and we don't know where the hell she is.

ELLEN DeGENERES

85

55

People often want to "get rid of" a "negative" emotion before attempting something new. That's the same thing as saying, "I want to get rid of some of my energy."

It's all right to have
butterflies in your stomach.
Just get them to fly in formation.

DR. ROB GILBERT

85

56

Fear, guilt, unworthiness, hurt feelings, and anger are, in fact, *tools*. Tools are neutral—they can be used *for* us, or *against* us. A knife can be used to heal or hurt. A hammer can be used to build or destroy. It is not the tool itself, but *the way the tool is used* that determines its benefit or detriment.

They shall beat their swords into plowshares,
and their spears into pruning hooks:
nation shall not lift up sword against nation,
neither shall they learn war any more.

ISAIAH 2:4

85

57

Imagine if all the energy of fear, guilt, unworthiness, hurt feelings, and anger were available to help us achieve anything we wanted.

Well, it is.

> *I know God will not give me*
> *anything I can't handle.*
> *I just wish that*
> *He didn't trust me so much.*
>
> MOTHER TERESA

86

58

It's as though someone hung a large rock around our neck. "Oh, how heavy," we'd complain. Later we were told the rock was really a diamond in the rough. "Oh! How heavy!" we'd exclaim. Fear, guilt, unworthiness, hurt feelings, and anger are diamonds in the rough. They're valuable now, and with a little cutting and polishing, they become priceless.

*We must select the illusion
which appeals to our temperament
and embrace it with passion,
if we want to be happy.*

CYRIL CONNOLLY

87

*When such as I cast out remorse
So great a sweetness flows into the breast
We must laugh and we must sing,
We are blest by everything,
Everything we look upon is blest.*

WILLIAM BUTLER YEATS

59

Fear is the energy to do your best in a new situation.

Try a thing you haven't done three times.
Once, to get over the fear of doing it.
Twice, to learn how to do it.
And a third time to figure out
whether you like it or not.

VIRGIL THOMSON

89

60

Contrary to popular belief, our parents didn't teach us to feel fear. Our parents *did* teach us to use fear as a reason *not* to do something. Children cannot logically determine whether their physical well-being is or is not endangered when attempting each new activity.

> *Society attacks early,*
> *when the individual is helpless.*
>
> B. F. SKINNER

89

61

Once you know something is not physically dangerous, go ahead and *do* the thing. It may feel uncomfortable (count on it), but keep moving one step after another in the direction of doing it.

As you move—as you *use it*—the energy will transform itself from barrier to blessing. You'll have *energy*, not limitation.

There are risks and costs to a program of action, but they are far less than the long-range risks and costs of comfortable inaction.

JOHN F. KENNEDY

91

62

Feeling the fear and doing it anyway reprograms our attitude from, "Fear means, 'Don't'" to "Fear means, 'All systems go!'"

You gain strength, courage and confidence
by every experience in which
you really stop to look fear in the face.
You are able to say to yourself,
"I lived through this horror.
I can take the next thing that comes along."
You must do the thing you think you cannot do.

ELEANOR ROOSEVELT

91

63

Guilt is the energy for personal change.

The wages of sin are death,
but by the time taxes are taken out,
it's just sort of a tired feeling.

PAULA POUNDSTONE

93

64

When we feel guilty and want to use the anger for change (for a change), we have two options: we can either change our *actions,* or change our *beliefs* about those actions.

> *Everything I did in my life*
> *that was worthwhile*
> *I caught hell for.*
>
> EARL WARREN

93

65

There's a lot of energy in the anger of guilt. It's a matter of remembering to redirect it from *blame* to *change—over and over.*

> *Destiny is not a matter of chance;*
> *it is a matter of choice.*
> *It is not a thing to be waited for;*
> *it is a thing to be achieved.*

WILLIAM JENNINGS BRYAN

95

66

When used to produce guilt, the statement, "I could have done better!" is false. If we *knew* better we'd *do* better.

A more accurate statement when we *intellectually* know better (and do it anyway) is to say, "This will remind me to do better next time—I'm still learning." Because, of course, we are.

Show me a guy who's afraid to look bad
and I'll show you a guy you can beat every time.

RENE AUBERJONOIS

97

67

Unworthiness keeps us on track.

> *There are three reasons why*
> *lawyers are replacing rats*
> *as laboratory research animals.*
> *One is that they're plentiful,*
> *another is that lab assistants*
> *don't get attached to them,*
> *and the third is that*
> *there are some things*
> *rats just won't do.*

99

68

Worthiness and unworthiness keep us on our path. It is our path. We selected it—it leads to our dream. Unworthiness is a friend that says, "Your path is this way, not that way." Be content knowing that your dream is yours, and accept that everything that's not your dream is not yours.

Seen in this way, the feeling of unworthiness is better described as humility. We know what we want, we know the direction we're going, we know that we are entitled to our dream, and we let the rest of the goals go by.

Being a newspaper columnist is like being married to a nymphomaniac. It's great for the first two weeks.

LEWIS GRIZZARD

101

69

Hurt feelings are a reminder of how much we care, and anger is the energy for change.

> *Don't go around saying*
> *the world owes you a living;*
> *the world owes you nothing;*
> *it was here first.*

MARK TWAIN

103

70

We only feel hurt about what we care about. Yes, when anger covers the hurt we say, "I don't care about them (it); I *hate* them (it)." That's part of caring, too.

Vex not thy spirit at the course of things;
they heed not thy vexation.
How ludicrous and outlandish is astonishment
at anything that may happen in life.

MARCUS AURELIUS

103

*Oh God,
in the name of Thine
only beloved Son,
Jesus Christ, Our Lord,
let him phone me <u>now</u>.*

DOROTHY PARKER

71

Another word for caring, of course, is **love**. Love is powerful. Keep it directed toward your goal. Most people use hurt as a reason to stop doing. If we let this happen, we truly **are** hurt; we hurt ourselves by letting hurt keep us from attaining our heart's desire.

When love and skill work together,
expect a masterpiece.

JOHN RUSKIN

103

72

Feel the *passion* of the caring. Put that passion behind your goal. If you feel *anger*, remember this is the energy for change. *Use* it; *do* something with it. Even if you can't do anything physically, use the passion to *imagine* success.

The ancestor of every action is a thought.

RALPH WALDO EMERSON

103

73

Our *feelings* don't say stop—our *programming* says stop. It's time to rewrite that programming to say, "Here's the information and the energy I need to make necessary corrections and continue moving toward my dreams."

Very few people possess true artistic ability.
It is therefore both unseemly and unproductive
to irritate the situation by making an effort.
If you have a burning, restless urge to write or paint,
simply eat something sweet and the feeling will pass.

FRAN LEBOWITZ

105

74

This is the power of the **imagination**: we can return to the past, rehearse the future, and zoom off on flights of fancy—all within seconds. The imagination is for rehearsing our dreams and reliving our joys.

I can believe anything,
provided it is incredible.

OSCAR WILDE

75

When the comfort zone has control of the imagination, it is vigorously and creatively used *against* us. We re-live the horrors of the past—fears that were justified, guilts that were especially foul, unworthinesses at their worst, hurt feelings at their most painful, anger at its most destructive.

*The longer I live the more I see
that I am never wrong about anything,
and that all the pains I have so humbly taken
to verify my notions have only wasted my time.*

GEORGE BERNARD SHAW

123

76

Evict it! Out! Your imagination is yours. You can re-member the past you choose, rehearse the future you want, relate to the real and fictional heroes and events you select, identify with the heroes you hold dear.

> *I am looking for a lot of men*
> *who have an infinite capacity*
> *to not know what can't be done.*

HENRY FORD

125

*The way you activate the seeds of your creation
is by making choices
about the results you want to create.
When you make a choice,
you mobilize vast human energies and resources
which otherwise go untapped.
All too often people fail to focus
their choices upon results
and therefore their choices are ineffective.
If you limit your choices only to
what seems possible or reasonable,
you disconnect yourself
from what you truly want,
and all that is left
is a compromise.*

ROBERT FRITZ

77

Often, what we *really* want is hidden beneath what we've settled for. When the comfort zone doesn't allow the expanded behavior necessary to fulfill our dream, we tend to forget the dream. It's too painful otherwise. When we know we *can* have what we want—that the comfort zone is under *our* control—we can remember what it is we truly want.

Poor is the man whose pleasures
depend on the permission of another.

MADONNA

141

78

An intention is what we want. **Methods** are the ways of getting it. An intention is our heart's desire. Methods are the *actions, information, things, and behaviors* we use to get it.

*Strong lives are motivated
by dynamic purposes.*

KENNETH HILDEBRAND

155

79

When you ask some people why they're not living their dream, they usually respond with a listing of unavailable methods: not enough money, looks, information, contacts, breaks, and so on. All these are just methods. Excuses of not having them may sound rational, but are, in reality, rational lies.

Perfections of means and confusion of goals seem
—in my opinion—
to characterize our age.

ALBERT EINSTEIN

155

80

Most people let their methods decide their intentions. This is a fundamental mistake. Those who look at what they already *have* before selecting what they *want* are involved in *making do,* not *doing*.

> *The great thing in this world*
> *is not so much where we are,*
> *but in what direction we are moving.*

OLIVER WENDELL HOLMES

155

81

The reason many people feel bored and unfulfilled is that they spend their lives shuffling and reshuffling the methods they already have. This can be like rearranging deck chairs on the *Titanic*—no matter how well it's done, the result is the same. As someone said, "If you do what you've always done, you'll get what you've always gotten."

One doesn't discover new lands without consenting to lose sight of the shore for a very long time.

ANDRÉ GIDE

155

Let's Get Off Our Buts

82

When choosing a dream, look to your heart, not to your "reality." That's why it's called a dream. Make that dream your intention. Commit to it. Act upon that commitment. The methods to fulfill that dream will appear.

Follow your bliss.

JOSEPH CAMPBELL

156

83

Selfing means doing for one's Self, in the larger sense of Self, as in True Self, or "To thine own self be true." It means fulfilling our inherent dreams, goals, and aspirations. It means living our life "on purpose."

This above all:
to thine own self be true,
And it must follow,
as the night the day,
Thou canst not then be false
to any man.

SHAKESPEARE

84

Selfish, on the other hand, describes the petty, end-lessly greedy gathering of stuff (houses, cars, boats, clothes), stuff (husbands, wives, children, lovers), and more stuff (power, fame, money, sex). It's the relentless pursuit of glamour at all costs. It's worshiping the god of other people's opinion.

> *The only man who is really free*
> *is the one who can turn down*
> *an invitation to dinner*
> *without giving an excuse.*

JULES RENARD

165

85

Selfing is knowing what you want—what *you* want, not what you *should* want because others *say* you should want it—and moving toward it.

Others may call you selfish, but you know that you are selfing—"being yourself."

We forfeit three-fourths of ourselves
to be like other people.

ARTHUR SCHOPENHAUER
(1788–1860)

165

86

You can have *anything* you want, but you can't have *everything* you want.

> *The important thing in acting*
> *is to be able to laugh and cry.*
> *If I have to cry,*
> *I think of my sex life.*
> *If I have to laugh,*
> *I think of my sex life.*

GLENDA JACKSON

87

You can have *anything* you want: No dream is too big to achieve. If *one other* person has achieved it, you can be the second. If *no other* person has achieved it, you can be the first. Dream big, dear reader, dream big.

If someone says "can't,"
that shows you what to do.

JOHN CAGE

169

88

But you can't have *everything* you want: We live in a finite world for a finite period of time, but with an infinite imagination. Our imagination can create more wants than a computer can generate random numbers. We're not going to have time for all the wants we want.

> *When the eagles are silent
> the parrots begin to jabber.*
>
> SIR WINSTON CHURCHILL

169

89

The biggest lie in choosing is "I can't."

It is simply not true.

The next time you hear yourself saying, to another—and especially to yourself—"I can't," take a deep breath and say instead, "My resources are otherwise engaged."

Because that's the truth.

Always do sober what you said you'd do drunk.
That will teach you to keep your mouth shut.

ERNEST HEMINGWAY

Let's Get Off Our Buts

90

When choosing a dream to pursue, it's good first to consider the four basic areas in which people live. They are

Marriage/Family
Career/Professional
Social/Political
Religious/Spiritual

Happiness?
A good cigar, a good meal,
and a good woman—or a bad woman.
It depends on how much happiness you can handle.

GEORGE BURNS

175

91

Naturally, in the course of a lifetime, people spend some time in each category. Looking back, however, most people can say, "Yes, I gave the majority of my time and attention to _____" and mention one of the categories. Sometimes, it's the area they *wanted* to spend most of their time in. Other times, they spent their life in an area *other* than the one closest to their heart.

> *Here is the test to find whether*
> *your mission on earth is finished.*
> *If you're alive, it isn't.*

RICHARD BACH

175

92

In choosing *now* which area you feel most drawn to, you can either (a) spend more time in that area, or (b) realize that the draw you feel ("I really *want* to do this, but I think I *should* do that") is from programming other than your own. Now is a good time to start reprogramming yourself so that the goals you follow are your own.

I once complained to my father that I didn't seem
to be able to do things the same way other people did.
Dad's advice?
"Margo, don't be a sheep.
People hate sheep. They eat sheep."

MARGO KAUFMAN

175

93

I'm not sure whether all work and no play made Jack a dull boy, or whether Jack was a dull boy to begin with, so, dullard that he was, he worked too much. Either way, **fun** and **recreation** are a necessary part of an undull life.

Lots of folks confuse bad management with destiny.

KIN HUBBARD

Cats are intended to teach us
that not everything in nature
has a function.

GARRISON KEILLOR

207

94

When I say *recreation*, I mean it in the lighter sense of recreation (tennis, boating, going to the movies), as well as in the deeper sense—*re-creation*. What do you do to "recreate" yourself? This might include meditation, retreats *(re-treats),* prayer, spiritual work, rest, pilgrimages, massage, silent time—whatever activities recharge your batteries in a deep and powerful way.

> *How beautiful it is to do nothing,*
> *and then rest afterward.*
>
> SPANISH PROVERB

207

95

It's important to realize, however, that the endless pursuit of fun and recreation *in and of themselves* is not very fulfilling. In fact, it's something of a curse. When one pursues pleasure *all the time*, the pursuit of pleasure becomes work—it's a job.

> *I can think of nothing less pleasurable*
> *than a life devoted to pleasure.*
>
> JOHN D. ROCKEFELLER, JR.

96

I didn't include Fun/Recreation in the other areas of life because I assume this is an area people will want to enjoy no matter what other area of life they choose. To use the battery analogy, Fun/Recreation charges the batteries; Marriage/Family, Career/Professional, Social/Political, and Religious/Spiritual are the ways in which the batteries are used.

> *The only true happiness*
> *comes from squandering ourselves*
> *for a purpose.*
>
> WILLIAM COWPER

97

Relationships are essential to the pursuit of almost any goal. In successfully pursuing a goal, however, it is important to understand the different types of relationships that are available. When you do, you can see which types of relationships can best help you pursue your dream.

A Code of Honor—Never approach a friend's
girlfriend or wife with mischief as your goal.
There are just too many women in the world
to justify that sort of dishonorable behavior.
Unless she's <u>really</u> attractive.

BRUCE JAY FRIEDMAN

211

98

Before exploring the types of relationships humans tend to have, here are two essential points about relationships in general. First, *all relationships are with yourself*—and sometimes they involve other people. Second, *the most important relationship in your life*—the one you'll have, like it or not, until the day you die—*is with yourself.*

> *Among those whom I like or admire,*
> *I can find no common denominator,*
> *but among those whom I love, I can:*
> *all of them make me laugh.*

W. H. AUDEN

211

99

Recreational Relationships: These are the people we enjoy being with simply because we enjoy being with them. *What* we do together is not as important as *that we are* together.

> *We don't love qualities.*
> *We love a person;*
> *sometimes by reason of their defects*
> *as well as their qualities.*

JACQUES MARITAIN

100

Romantic Relationships: Here, sex—or sexual desire—combines with a feeling of "you are the only one for me," and "if you don't love me, I'm miserable and worthless." We don't have to like—or even know—the "love object." Some say ignorance is a prerequisite for romantic love.

Of course it is possible to love a human being,
if you don't know them too long.

CHARLES BUKOWSKI

212

101

Contractual Relationships: In a contractual relationship, something is exchanged for something else. The "something" could be anything—a product, a service, an experience. Usually the culturally agreed upon symbol for energy—money—is involved in the transaction.

> *Almost all of our relationships begin*
> *and most of them continue*
> *as forms of mutual exploitation,*
> *a mental or physical barter,*
> *to be terminated when*
> *one or both parties run out of goods.*

W. H. AUDEN

215

102

Common-Goal Relationships: Here people share a common goal, and that goal is the primary reason they relate. This is often the source of work-based relationships. The common goal may be a company goal, a personal goal fulfilled by the company, or simply, as Sir Noel Coward put it, "your pay packet at the end of the week."

The value of marriage is not
that adults produce children,
but that children produce adults.

PETER DE VRIES

215

103

Power-Point Relationships: This is a specific form of common-goal relationship. Here one person becomes the "power point." A group feeds its energy (power) to the power-point person, and through this power point, the entire group can fulfill its common goal.

If the point is sharp, and the arrow is swift,
it can pierce through the dust no matter how thick.

BOB DYLAN

104

There are few "pure" relationships—most cross lines, combining one type of relationship with another. Relationships also change over time, evolving—or deteriorating—from one type to another.

My parents have been visiting me for a few days.
I just dropped them off at the airport.
They leave tomorrow.

MARGARET SMITH

219

*I've been promoted to middle management.
I never thought I'd sink so low.*

TIM GOULD

*Never keep up with the Joneses.
Drag them down to your level.
It's cheaper.*

QUENTIN CRISP

*I don't know much about
being a millionaire,
but I'll bet I'd be <u>darling</u> at it.*

DOROTHY PARKER

105

Money, fame, and power—for their own sake—all spell one thing: *glamour.*

Glamour is one of the biggest traps in life. It is a sweet, sticky snare, like the petals of a Venus-flytrap. "Come to me," it beckons. "All happiness lies within."

> *What's money? A man is a success*
> *if he gets up in the morning*
> *and goes to bed at night*
> *and in between does what he wants to do.*

BOB DYLAN

243

I travel light;
as light, that is,
as a man can travel
who will still
carry his body around
because of its sentimental value.

CHRISTOPHER FRY

106

Am I saying money, fame, and power are intrinsically evil? No. They have their place. They are tools—*methods* for obtaining goals. As goals themselves, however, they are nothing. Less than nothing. Distractions at best; addictions at worst.

A celebrity is a person who
works hard all his life
to become well known,
then wears dark glasses
to avoid being recognized.

FRED ALLEN

243

107

Elementary school
$2 + 2 = 4$

College
$E = mc^2$

Life
TIME = DREAMS

Men, for the sake of getting a living, forget to live.

MARGARET FULLER

253

108

What do you want?

> *What would you attempt to do*
> *if you knew you could not fail?*
>
> ### DR. ROBERT SHULLER

257

109

Put something countable, something quantifiable in your goal so that you'll *know* when you've obtained it. You are not saddled with this goal forever and ever. When you reach it, you can choose a bigger one. For now, however, it's important to know *what* your goal is and be able to tell *when* you've reach it.

> *You've got to be very careful*
> *if you don't know where you are going,*
> *because you might not get there.*

YOGI BERRA

110

In order to have something new, we must expand our comfort zone to include the new thing. The bigger the new thing, the more the comfort zone must expand. And *comfort zones are most often expanded through discomfort.*

> *Do not be too timid and squeamish*
> *about your actions.*
> *All life is an experiment.*

RALPH WALDO EMERSON

287

111

Committing to a dream is not a one-time occurrence. It must done daily, hourly, continually. We must *choose* to commit to our *choice*, over and over.

*In the afternoons, Gertrude Stein and I used to go
antique hunting in the local shops,
and I remember once asking her
if she thought I should become a writer.
In the typically cryptic way we were all enchanted with,
she said, "No."
I took that to mean yes
and sailed for Italy the next day.*

WOODY ALLEN

290

112

The test of this commitment is action. If we say, "I commit to being a great dancer," and then don't practice, that's not a commitment; that's not dance; that's just talk.

Never take a solemn oath.
People think you mean it.

NORMAN DOUGLAS

291

113

When we commit and act, we are confronted by the comfort zone. We are tempted to stop, encouraged to stop, *demanded* to stop. If we move ahead *anyway*—we expand the comfort zone, learn a necessary lesson, and the commitment becomes stronger. That causes us to come up against the comfort zone again, and the process continues. Yes, it's uncomfortable, but (a) you'll get what you want and (b) in addition to what you want, you'll have an expanded comfort zone.

If you never want to see a man again, say,
"I love you, I want to marry you.
I want to have children . . ."
—they leave skid marks.

RITA RUDNER

291

114

Here are some suggestions for making and keeping commitments:

1. Don't make commitments you don't plan to keep.
2. Learn to say no.
3. Make conditional agreements. ("If . . . then . . .")
4. Keep the commitments you make.
5. Write commitments down. (Keep a calendar.)
6. If conflicts arise, renegotiate at the earliest opportunity.

Eighty percent of success is showing up.

WOODY ALLEN

291

Until one is committed,
there is hesitancy,
the chance to draw back,
always ineffectiveness.
Concerning all acts of initiative
(and creation)
There is one elementary truth,
the ignorance of which
kills countless ideas and splendid plans:
that the moment one definitely commits oneself,
then Providence moves too.
All sorts of things occur to help one
that would never otherwise have occurred.

*A whole stream of events
issues from the decision,
raising in one's favor
all manner of unforeseen incidents
and meetings and material assistance,
which no man could have dreamed
would have come his way.*

*I have learned a deep respect
for one of Goethe's couplets:*

**Whatever you can do, or dream you can, begin it.
Boldness has genius, power and magic in it.**

W. H. MURRAY
THE SCOTTISH HIMALAYAN EXPEDITION

115

It's important to commit to the fulfillment of the goal, not just to a certain amount of time spent pursuing the goal. When we commit to *pursuing*, our goal is then pursuing, and we will pursue. We won't necessarily get what we're pursuing, because getting it is not our goal—pursuing it is.

I always wanted to be somebody,
but I should have been more specific.

LILY TOMLIN

297

116

The time to commit is now.

   And now.

      And now.

        And now.

          And now.

            And now.

              And now.

                And now.

                  And now . . .

297

117

Keep your goals away from the trolls.

*It is a mistake for a sculptor or a painter
to speak or write very often about his job.
It releases the tension needed for his work.*

HENRY MOORE

*Give not which is holy unto the dogs,
neither cast ye your pearls before swine,
lest they trample them under their feet,
and turn again and rend you.*

JESUS OF NAZARETH
MATTHEW 7:6

299

118

People don't like to see others pursuing their dreams—
it reminds them how far from living their dreams they
are. In talking you out of your dreams, they are talking
themselves back into their own comfort zone. They will
give you every rational lie they ever gave themselves.

> *These are the soul cages.*
> *These are the soul cages.*
> *Swim to the light.*
>
> STING

301

119

When you've obtained your goal, *then* tell others about it. Even though faced with irrefutable evidence, the most common expression you'll hear will be "I don't believe it!" If they can't believe reality, imagine how much difficulty they'd have believing in your Dream.

> *Losers visualize the penalties of failures.*
> *Winners visualize the rewards of success.*

DR. ROB GILBERT

301

120

To **affirm** is to *make firm*. An affirmation is a statement of truth you make firm by repetition. Affirmations help you believe in your Dream. Belief is essential. Your Dream must become more real than your doubt. Affirmations are like lifting weights—a mechanical process that helps build strength (belief) in your Dream.

I used to work at the The International House of Pancakes. It was a dream, and I made it happen.

PAULA POUNDSTONE

313

Your automatic creative mechanism
operates in terms of goals and end results.
Once you give it a definite goal to achieve,
you can depend on its automatic guidance system
to take you to that goal much better
than "You" ever could by conscious thought.
"You" supply the goal
by thinking in terms of end results.
Your automatic mechanism
then supplies the means whereby.

MAXWELL MALTZ

121

That our heroes became heroes *flaws and all* gives us hope. "You mean we don't have to be perfect to fulfill our Dream, to make a contribution?" Hardly. It takes commitment, courage, and passion to live a dream and make a contribution. Heroes had these qualities *along with* their flaws. And you have those qualities, too.

Have I ever told you you're my hero?
You're everything I would like to be.
I can climb higher than an eagle.
You are the wind beneath my wings.

LARRY HENLEY
JEFF SILBAR

321

122

Within our bodies is the energy of individual creation. We call this **achievement energy.** People experience achievement energy differently depending on what they call it. Just as a certain energy in the body can be called "fear" or "excitement," so, too, the energy of achievement can be called *creative, sexual,* or *spiritual*.

> *Creativity can solve almost any problem.*
> *The creative act,*
> *the defeat of habit by originality,*
> *overcomes everything.*

GEORGE LOIS

327

123

When we direct this energy of achievement toward anything, it becomes *passion*. Most people have their passion hard-wired (and often hot-wired) in a particular direction. It might be a person, certain foods, a TV program, sex, money, football, macramé—whatever.

Success is not the result of spontaneous combustion.
You must set yourself on fire.

REGGIE LEACH

353

*You can have anything you want
if you want it desperately enough.
You must want it with an inner exuberance
that erupts through the skin
and joins the energy that created the world.*

SHEILA GRAHAM

124

What we feel passionate about is our choice. For most of us, however, the choice was made long ago. We *know* what the choice is—whatever we automatically feel passionate about—but we've forgotten having made the choice.

*Put all your eggs
in one basket and*
WATCH THAT BASKET!

MARK TWAIN

353

If you have built castles in the air,
your work need not be lost;
that is where they should be.
Now put the foundations under them.

HENRY DAVID THOREAU

The hand is the cutting edge of the mind.

JACOB BRONOWSKI

125

You can, however, redirect the passion from something you currently feel passionate about to your Dream at any point. All it takes is (a) remembering to do it, and (b) a *specific* image to feel passionate about.

> *One person with belief*
> *is equal to a force of*
> *ninety-nine who have only interests.*

JOHN STUART MILL

354

126

The biggest lie we tell ourselves in the area of action is, "I'll do it later."

Delay is the deadliest form of denial.
C. NORTHCOTE PARKINSON

369

127

The interesting thing about "later" is that a statement containing it can never be proven false. One can never reproach us for not doing something. If confronted, we can always say, "I said I'd do it later. It's not later yet."

If you trap the moment before it's ripe,
The tears of repentance you'll certainly wipe;
But if once you let the ripe moment go
You can never wipe off the tears of woe.

WILLIAM BLAKE

369

128

If you can do something now, do it now. If it can't be done now, (a) decide if it's going to be done. If yes, (b) choose *when* it will get done.

Laziness is nothing more than the habit of resting before you get tired.

JULES RENARD

129

A primary reason people don't do new things is because they want to do them perfectly—first time. It's irrational, impractical, unworkable—and yet, it's how most people run their lives. It's called The Perfection Syndrome.

Have no fear of perfection—you'll never reach it.

SALVADOR DALI

373

130

Whoever said we had to do it perfect? (Just DO IT!)

When in doubt, make a fool of yourself.
There is a microscopically thin line
between being brilliantly creative and
acting like the most gigantic idiot on earth.
So what the hell, leap.

CYNTHIA HEIMEL

373

131

Enough! It's time to grow up. If we want to play adult games—living our Dream—we must play by adult rules. One of the primary adult rules: We are individually responsible for our own lives.

Creativity represents a miraculous coming together
of the uninhibited energy of the child
with its apparent opposite and enemy,
the sense of order imposed on
the disciplined adult intelligence.

NORMAN PODHORETZ

389

132

Responsibility simply means, "The ability to respond." In any of life's challenges, opportunities, or disasters, we can *respond* in whatever way we choose. It's not a matter of right/wrong, good/bad. It's a matter of *practical analysis* of the situation.

There's nothing to winning, really.
That is, if you happen to be blessed with
a keen eye, an agile mind,
and no scruples whatsoever.

ALFRED HITCHCOCK

389

133

In addition to what we can do *physically* about a situation, we also have the ability to choose what our *inner* response to that situation is.

> *The greatest discovery of my generation
> is that a human being can alter his life by
> altering his attitudes of mind.*

> WILLIAM JAMES
> (1842–1910)

390

134

This is a big one. It sounds like a radical new idea, but it's not. It's centuries old. The idea is this: we control our emotional *reaction* to the external environment— the external environment doesn't.

If you are distressed by anything external,
the pain is not due to the thing itself,
but to your estimate of it;
and this you have the power to revoke at any moment.

MARCUS AURELIUS

390

135

It is OK to feel good when things go bad. Being content, satisfied, and joyful no matter *what* happens is a radical concept—but it's also a basic rule of adult life.

An Englishman thinks he is moral
when he is only uncomfortable.

GEORGE BERNARD SHAW

When I was born
I was so surprised
I didn't talk
for a year and a half.

GRACIE ALLEN

391

136

We don't plan to fail, we just fail to plan. So, plan. And be prepared not just to change *horses* in midstream, but to change to a *boat* in midstream. Keep your goal, your Dream. Stay firm and fixed on that. Be prepared, however, for whatever methods come along to get you there. *Especially* methods not on your plan. Plan on it.

> *Next week there can't be any crisis.*
> *My schedule is already full.*

HENRY A. KISSINGER

395

137

Someone once said, "A blank sheet of paper is God's way of letting you know what it feels like to be God." So is a blank calendar. A calendar for the next year represents your *time,* one of the most precious commodities you have. Use it well. Choosing what you want to do, and when to do it, is an act of creation. You are creating your Dream.

> *I've been on a calendar,*
> *but I've never been on time.*
>
> MARILYN MONROE

399

A lot of successful people are risk-takers.
Unless you're willing to do that,
to have a go,
to fail miserably,
and have another go,
success won't happen.

PHILIP ADAMS

138

As often as successful people counsel us to "take risks," that's about how often we ignore such counsel. For the vast, vast majority of people, taking risks is just too, well, *risky*. If we don't take risks, however, it's doubtful we'll ever get to our Dream.

Once you accept your own death,
all of a sudden
you're free to live.
You no longer care about your reputation.
You no longer care except so far as
your life can be used tactically—
to promote a cause you believe in.

SAUL ALINKSKY

403

139

The irony is that the person *not* taking risks feels the same amount of fear as the person who *regularly* takes risks. The non-risk-taker simply feels the *same* amount of fear over *trivial* things.

> *Every man has the right*
> *to risk his own life*
> *in order to save it.*

JEAN-JACQUES ROUSSEAU

404

140

People not taking calculated risks in pursuing their Dream sometimes take foolish risks in general. They drive too fast, drink too much, abuse drugs, or engage in some other reckless behavior.

Take calculated risks.
That is quite different from being rash.

GEORGE PATTON

A cardinal rule of politics—
never get caught in bed with a live man or a dead woman.

J. R. EWING
DALLAS

404

141

When we commit to a goal, the methods to achieve that goal will appear. When the methods do appear, they may not be (and seldom are) dressed in familiar garb. Many people are in the habit of saying "no" to all new experiences. Don't say no till you know what you're saying no to.

*The greatest obstacle to discovery is not ignorance—
it is the illusion of knowledge.*

DANIEL J. BOORSTIN

407

142

Your goal-fulfillment system is working all the time—pulling experiences, lessons, information, and people to you to help you fulfill your Dream.

Let your hook always be cast.
In the pool where you least expect it, will be a fish.

OVID

411

143

Mistakes show us what we need to learn. They indicate what we must study in order to have success. When we make a mistake, it's a golden arrow saying, "Study this if you want success."

From error to error, one discovers the entire truth.

SIGMUND FREUD

413

144

Many people read about the value of mistakes, say, "That makes sense," and then continue living their lives in the same avoid-mistakes-at-all-costs manner as before. They continue to play it safe, don't learn what they need to know, and then wonder why they're not closer to their Dream.

Try everything once
except incest and folk dancing.

SIR THOMAS BEECHAM

413

Inside the ears of crazy people:

Go to the zoo and enlist.
Shave your neighbor's dog.
Yo! Dump your spaghetti on that guy's head.

GARY LARSON

I owe my success to
having listened respectfully
to the very best advice,
and then going away
and doing the exact opposite.

G. K. CHESTERTON

145

The process of learning can be summarized in four steps:

1. Act.
2. Look for the mistakes (criticize, evaluate).
3. Learn how to do it better next time.
4. Go to 1.

You will make all kinds of mistakes;
but as long as you are generous and true,
and also fierce,
you cannot hurt the world
or even seriously distress her.

SIR WINSTON CHURCHILL

415

146

Distractions do not bring satisfaction. Let go of them. A distraction is anything not on the way to our goal that consumes our time, thoughts, or emotional energy.

The sun will set without thy assistance.

THE TALMUD

417

147

The distractions do *anything they want* to tempt you off your path: offer sex, food, fame, power, success in an area not part of your Dream, recognition, easy money— *anything*. What they *cannot* do is get *on* your path and *stop you*. Leaving the path is always *your choice*. Pursue your Dream. Follow your path.

> *Never give in.*
> *Never. Never. Never. Never.*

SIR WINSTON CHURCHILL

148

Your job is to fulfill your Dream.

> *My philosophy is that*
> *not only are you responsible*
> *for your life,*
> *but doing the best*
> *at this moment*
> *puts you in the best place*
> *for the next moment.*

OPRAH WINFREY

419

Let's Get Off Our Buts

149

Pursuing your Dream requires work—mental, emotional, and physical. Work is what we don't want to do, but we do anyway to get something else. To reach your Dream, you'll have to do a lot of things you don't want to do.

*Opportunity is missed by most people
because it is dressed in overalls
and looks like work.*

THOMAS EDISON

439

150

How do we know when we've done enough work? When we have what we want, it was enough. Until then, it wasn't. Do the work until it's enough—until you have your Dream.

Do something every day that you don't want to do.
This is the golden rule for acquiring
the habit of doing your duty without pain.

MARK TWAIN

441

154

People, books, tapes, videos, magazines, etc. are all shortcuts to success.

Learn from the accumulated wisdom of the ages. That's what it's been accumulating for.

The journey of ten thousand miles
begins with a single phone call.

CONFUCIUS BELL

453

153

Keep track of your successes—the achievement of the interim goals on the way to the Big One. As this list grows, it becomes a testament to your power, your creativity, your achievement. (Besides, in the years to come, your many biographers will appreciate whatever help you can give them.)

Writing is easy.
All you do is stare at a blank sheet of paper
until drops of blood form on your forehead.

GENE FOWLER

451

152

Nothing is impossible. The more improbable something is, however, the more work it takes to achieve.

The one unchangeable certainty is that nothing is unchangeable or certain.

JOHN F. KENNEDY

447

151

Consider the pursuit of your dream a major athletic event. Train for it. What we exercise gets stronger. That's true mentally, emotionally, and physically.

Physically: Keep fit.

Emotions: Keep them flexible.

Mind: Keep it open.

Comfort Zone: Keep expanding it.

*Only Irish coffee provides in a single glass
all four essential food groups:
alcohol, caffeine, sugar, and fat.*

ALEX LEVINE

443

155

In following *your* Dream, you will probably notice that you have more rules than ever before. What's going on? Isn't your Dream supposed to bring *freedom?* Yes, and freedom is found in discipline.

In the last analysis,
our only freedom
is the freedom
to discipline ourselves.

BERNARD BARUCH

455

156

Discipline comes from the word *disciple*—being a devoted student. Think of discipline as a container. Once a container is constructed—and maintained—it can envelop your Dream.

Take what you can use
and let the rest go by.

KEN KESEY

455

157

Begin to formulate your own set of "rules" on how *you* best achieve dreams. To fulfill our Dream, we need only examine our life, and do two things:

1. More of what works.
2. Less of what doesn't.

I've got to keep breathing.
It'll be my worst business mistake if I don't.

SIR NATHAN MEYER ROTHSCHILD

158

It's important to nurture yourself while you're nurturing your Dream. In the large sense, of course, pursuing your Dream *is* nurturing yourself. Along the way to your Dream, however, take time to be good to yourself.

> *I'm at an age where I think*
> *more about food than sex.*
> *Last week I put a mirror*
> *over my dining room table.*

RODNEY DANGERFIELD

459

Let's Get Off Our Buts

159

Succumbing to the comfort zone's demands is *not* "taking care of yourself." Nurturing yourself means taking care of yourself *while you do what needs to be done.* This might mean working twenty hours on a project you *could* complete in fifteen. It does *not* mean not doing the project.

Advice to expectant mothers: you must remember that
when you are pregnant, you are eating for two.
But you must remember that the other one of you
is about the size of a golf ball, so let's not go overboard with it.
I mean, a lot of pregnant women eat as though
the other person they're eating for is Orson Welles.

DAVE BARRY

459

160

Rehabilitate your attitude toward words such as "work," "vacation" and "time off." The idea that we need "time off" comes from working for another to fulfill another's dreams. Now your life is directed toward fulfilling *your* Dream. Why would you want to take "time off" from that?

INTERVIEWER:
Your Holiness, how many people work in the Vatican?

POPE JOHN XXIII:
About half.

459

161

Learn to seek *satisfaction* in a job well done, rather than seek diversion in activities designed to distract you from the "harsh reality of work."

I don't have anything against work.
I just figure, why deprive somebody who really loves it?

DOBIE GILLIS

The more I want to get something done,
the less I call it work.

RICHARD BACH

460

162

True nurturing is learning to enjoy the path, the process, the journey toward your Dream.

> *If A is success in life,*
> *then A equals X plus Y plus Z.*
> *Work is X,*
> *Y is play,*
> *and Z is keeping your mouth shut.*
>
> ALBERT EINSTEIN

> *Keep walking and keep smiling.*
>
> TINY TIM

460

163

Nothing succeeds like **persistence**. The common denominator of *all* successful people is their persistence.

Nothing in the world can take the place of persistence.
Talent will not;
nothing is more common than unsuccessful men with talent.
Genius will not;
unrewarded genius is almost a proverb.
Education alone will not;
the world is full of educated derelicts.
Persistence and determination alone are omnipotent.

CALVIN COOLIDGE

463

164

Persistence is a simple process:

1. What's the next step?
2. What's in the way of taking that step?
3. Remove, disregard, or ignore the obstacle.
4. Take the step.
5. Go to 1.

Fall seven times, stand up eight.
JAPANESE PROVERB

165

Rather than "comfort and joy," try *enthusiasm* and joy. Enthusiam and joy are Siamese twins—it's hard to find one without the other. Enthusiasm comes from the Latin *en theos*—one with the energy of the Divine. The way to create joy is to do things joyfully.

The real secret of success is enthusiasm.

WALTER CHRYSLER

467

166

When your Dream is *almost* realized—but not quite—it's time to choose another goal.

Saddle your dreams afore you ride 'em.

MARY WEBB
(1881–1927)

471

167

When we know how easy it is to fulfill a Dream (easy compared to how *impossible* most people believe it to be), we know we *can* take the Dream for our own. Once we are free to take it, we are free to leave it.

A man is rich in proportion to the number of things which he can afford to let alone.

HENRY DAVID THOREAU

475

168

After fulfilling a Dream or two (or twenty), we will be called upon to pass on some of what we have learned to others. Just as, "When the student is ready, the teacher appears," so, too, "When the teacher is ready, the student appears."

> *We are here on earth to do good to others.*
> *What the others are here for; I don't know.*

W. H. AUDEN

477

169

After obtaining several material Dreams, you may wonder, "Where are these Dreams coming from?" Important question. Seeking the answer to that question may begin an important inner quest. What we learn from fulfilling Dreams in the outer world can be used for pursuing Dreams within ourselves.

*To know oneself
one should assert oneself.*

ALBERT CAMUS

481

170

When things are going awful, terrible, horrible, it helps to remember that, in six months, you'll be telling this "tragedy" as an anecdote.

> *Humor is an affirmation of dignity,*
> *a declaration of man's superiority*
> *to all that befalls him.*
>
> ROMAIN GARY

485

171

Humor is truth, truth is humor. By remembering that truth in the middle of the chaos, you can take a deep breath and say to yourself, "This is funny."

Humor is emotional chaos
remembered in emotional tranquility.

JAMES THURBER

485

172

Allow me to close with this from Guillaume Apollinaire—

"Come to the edge," he said.
They said, "We are afraid."
"Come to the edge," he said.
They came.
He pushed them
And they flew.

*For more information on
our books and unabridged audio tapes,
please write to*

*Prelude Press
8159 Santa Monica Boulevard
Los Angeles, CA 90046*

or call

1-800-LIFE-101

Thank You!

Index

Here I am
at the end of the road,
at the top of the heap.

POPE JOHN XXIII

WE WANT TO TELL YOU ABOUT OUR OTHER BOOKS!

Please send us your name and address so we can tell you about other Prelude Press books and audio tapes.

 Please place me on your mailing list.

 Please send free catalog.

 Please send free audio sampler tape.

NAME_____

ADDRESS_____

CITY_____STATE_____ZIP_____